Things About Small Business I Learned From My Parents

Written by

Catherine Ymbong-Ancheta

Copyright © 2021 Catherine Ymbong-Ancheta

All rights reserved.

No part of this book may be used or reproduced in any manner whatsoever without written permission except in the case of brief quotations embodied in critical articles or reviews.

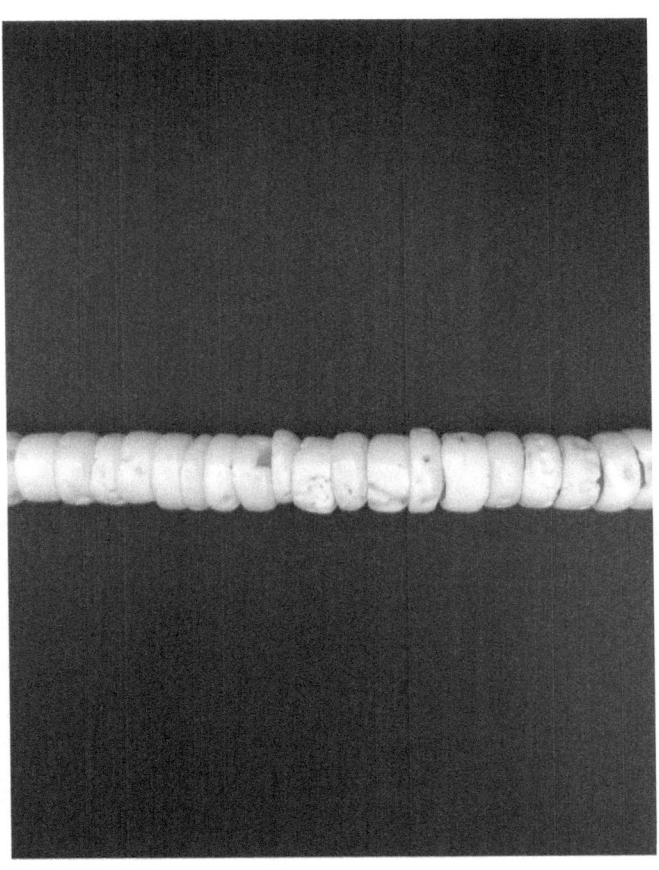

Puka Shells

Table of Contents

I-Sometimes You Find the Business, Sometimes It Finds You   1

II-Being a Manufacturer, a Wholesaler or a Retailer   7

III-Customer is Always Right   13

IV-Suppliers are as Important as Buyers   17

V-The Power of Prayer   21

VI-What Hat Do You Wear?   25

VII-Blending Traditional Ways With Modern Ways   29

VIII-Starting Business From Scratch   31

IX-Coming Full Circle   35

I

Sometimes You Find the Business, Sometimes It Finds You

I grew up in shellcraft-handicraft business in Cebu, Philippines. My parents, Frunnie and Jun, were among the pioneers in the industry during the 1970s. Philippines is an archipelago with over 7,000 islands and it might be inevitable that a business like this would come about. People gather shells and sell them to warehouses, who sell them to factories, who process them into beads or ornaments then sell them to traders, who sell them to foreigners who come to buy them and sell them wholesale in their countries or retail to beach tourists in places like Hawaii.

My parents set up a factory with about 100 workers, and many of those workers were recruited from a nearby province. Which required that my parents also had to provide separate living quarters for those ladies and men to sleep in and a sizeable kitchen and dining area for everyone. It was like family inside the factory. You can picture our factory not a big building, but a structure well built from bamboos, wood and coconut palms, with concrete flooring. It was large enough for the different sections of production. There was an area for "cutters," mostly they were young kids who wanted to earn extra allowance, myself included. We would cut shells into small sizes enough to make beads, using handy cutters. Bigger shells were cut by "slicers" using machines. Then those cut shells would go to the driller section. The "drillers" would make holes on those shells using electric tools. These drilled shell beads would be strung on wires so they could be tumbled in the machine to be polished, then buffed. This process would take place in the back section of the factory because there would be chemicals and dusts involved. Then, those beads would go to the long tables in the "necklacers" section where beads were put on nylon strings and designed for necklaces.

How my parents stumbled into this business was accidental. Somebody came to our house carrying puka beads. These are beads that come from the crown of cone shells and were very popular then. The man told my mother he was in the neighborhood looking to sell them and one neighbor told him Frunnie would buy them. It was a predicament some neighbor put my mother into. My mother told him she didn't know anything about those puka beads and if she would buy them, she wouldn't know whom to sell them to either. At that time, my mother was selling merchandise goods in our "*sari-sari*" store at home. The man told her there was this buyer in this hotel, who would buy those puka beads. She would just go to the hotel, ask for this foreign buyer by name, which the man gave my mother, and the buyer would pay her. He even told her at what price it would be bought, which was interesting enough for my mother to give it a try. Plus, my mother could even just pay the man later after she got the money. Unknown to her, this period was the "gold rush" in the shell beads industry.

And that was the beginning of my parents' business. Mama would consider this shellcraft business as a gift from above, as she had absolutely no idea who sent that man and why he came to find her. She and my father had run a few businesses before this. They had sold women's stockings, traded cigarettes, operated bus transportation, and ran a small merchandise store from home. Not all of these businesses were meant to be. When they were running buses, my mother often felt nervous that the doctor told her that if she wanted to live longer, she would have to find another business. My mother lived until 75 years old.

II

Being a Manufacturer, a Wholesaler or a Retailer

My parents operated the factory for a few years, like the others. There were a handful, however, who still kept their factories thirty years later. When orders were getting low and the cost of operating the factory -- electricity, equipment maintenance, and weekly salaries -- became a burden, my parents pivoted into wholesaling. The tools and machineries they either sold or lent to individual craftsmen who would take orders from them and make the products for them this time. Eventually, our workers had to go back to their hometowns. At this time, many wanted to settle down or find better careers, so the factory closure was accepted with great understanding. Life was simpler then.

As wholesalers, whenever my parents got orders from retailers, they would go to small factory shops and ordered more quantity of the item. Especially when dealing with small manufacturers, it was common to give a cash advance, so the manufacturer could buy the raw materials to start with. This manufacturer might even have to also set aside some money to give as a cash advance to his or her workers to lure them to work. Small manufacturers usually wouldn't have enough capital, so wholesalers had to take the risk. Sometimes, the money would be spent by the small factory owner on something else other than on the production of my parents' purchase order instead. By the time my parents would check on the scheduled delivery, it would be a lot less than the quantity expected or there might be no delivery at all. Rather, another promise of a new delivery date. One way to fix this was for my parents to purchase the raw materials themselves initially, and when the supplier made the delivery, the amount payable would be deducted. Of course, in dealing with some suppliers, they had to be checked upon before the delivery date too, to make sure they wouldn't be delivering the goods to other people which would leave the wholesale buyers cheated.

Another risk my parents faced as wholesalers involved delayed payments from their customers. When I was a small kid, I remembered this buyer from Manila who really stressed my mother because he wasn't paying. Either he would evade my mother's long-distance calls, or if my mother would travel to find him, he would make endless excuses. Why my mother trusted him, was because he started as a well-paying customer. Then orders became bigger, and then it happened. Sometimes, though, because my parents wanted to help their buyers with payments, they would take risk getting installment payments or accept post-dated checks. If both parties were sincere about doing business, that could work.

Perhaps because of my parents' exposure to retail shops where they often delivered handcrafted goods, and the travails of having to make deliveries, deal with quality control scrutiny, and having to follow-up payments, my mother convinced my father that they would start their own handicraft retail store. In 1983, they opened our first handicraft store in a newly built commercial center. It was a very well-sized store that my mother was surprised to find that despite the large inventory she purchased for its opening, the store still looked "empty" after they displayed the items. So, my mother passionately bought more goods to fill the store, until she felt it looked it had enough goods to sell. It was important for my mother then, and I begin to understand her point now whenever I pass by a newly opened shop and I do not feel enticed to go in because the store just looks so spacious and the items seem so few. After that one store, my parents were inspired to open another one, this time just selling raw seashells for collectors. Then another stall. And another stall in the city's popular market.

My mother had this vision of receiving a good income daily as she had not just one but a few stores. At the start -- especially when people hired to man the store and take charge of the cash register were still eager to make a good impression -- things ran smoothly. But because my mother would be so busy that she could only rely on the loyalty of the salesgirls and cashiers, she couldn't be sure anymore. At times, our store employees would reason that we just didn't have what the buyers were looking for, items that my mother had overlooked and failed to purchase. Later, when sales slowed down, the space rent would then be a nightmare. There were times my parents felt they were only working for the building lessor.

What changed my parents' focus was the novelty of joining retail trade shows where they made good money at the start. But then again, after a few years of doing trade shows that put a strain on my father's health, my parents came to feel that they were only working for the trade show organizers who charged seemingly exorbitant fees.

III

Customer is Always Right

Unless they renege on their payments, customers are always right. They should be treated special. My mother learned this the hard way early on in the business. In those days when telephones with rotating dials were still attached to wires and at times lacked dial tones, my parents had the privilege of using our close neighbor's phone if our home phone had problems. One morning while we were having breakfast, our generous neighbor let us know somebody had called long-distance, asking for my mother. She gave the name, and it was my parents' buyer. My mother was enjoying the breakfast that she wanted to finish and did not expect to be disturbed as to have to go to our neighbor's house for the phone. She sent a message to the neighbor she had to finish her meal and she could not take the call. This was a well-paying, good-mannered buyer who, at that time, would be considered their biggest client and who was ordering regularly. That was the end of it.

The buyer didn't want to talk to my mother anymore nor accept her call. She did not pursue him. The man was too hurt. Not even the good quality puka shell beads shipped on time to his company could make him look back. It would have been one of the best buyer-supplier relationships that could have seen many successes together. My mother so regretted it for many years. But of course, she moved on and learned that lesson big time.

When you are doing retail and sell directly to end-users, you please customers by making them feel they are getting a good, if not the best, product from you and they get it at the best price. When you are a manufacturer or wholesaler who sells to another businessman, you please the businessman customer by delivering the right goods, quality-wise and price-wise, on time. Also, communication is important. You have to make the customers feel that they are being listened to.

Enthusiasm is also important. When you sell with enthusiasm, it will rub off on the customers, making them more likely to buy. You have to believe in your product, and that sincere faith will make people want to try. And when the sale is made, make them feel they made the right decision and your dedication to them has remained.

IV

Suppliers are as Important as Buyers

People keep their business not just because they continue to have customers. Equally important are suppliers -- people who provide you the goods or services if you are a wholesaler or retailer, or people who provide you the raw materials for production if you are a manufacturer.

My parents had kept a journal that recorded information regarding their suppliers. Often, it came in handy when they needed a particular product, as they could reconnect with someone who made this item, even if they hadn't encountered this person in a long while. If that person had changed phone number or address, the journal would still provide information about other suppliers who might know the current phone number or address of the sought supplier, or similar supplier.

Throughout the years my parents were in business and they having met so many contacts who supplied them goods or services, there were only a handful of people who my parents could say were consistently on time and consistently supplied quality products or services. Indeed, these people were like gems in a heap of stones. Without these gems of a supplier, a business could not provide the goods and services it sought to continue to deliver to the customers. So, my parents also gave them the same attention and kind treatment they gave to buyers.

Yes, a business thrives on relationships. I learned later, in China they call it *guanxi*. In the Philippines, the closest term I could equate this to would be *pakikisama*, which captures the essence of good social manners, networking and sincerity. If you have money to start a small business but don't relate to other people well, it would be a very rough sail. On the contrary, I have seen people who didn't have enough capital or had prior business losses but were able to start a small business because of the honest-to-goodness relationships they had built with both suppliers and customers.

In the small business industry I grew up in, I had seen that taking time to show interest and make small conversations with employees, or suppliers and buyers allows you to see their worlds beyond your business relationships -- their children, their stories about their family; their health, important events, or financial goals and unique challenges – which are just as important as your discussions regarding product specifications and timelines. Why? Because people are motivated by the things that matter to them. Productivity, performance and production timelines in business actually could be influenced by the dynamics going on in the personal lives of people involved. Astute businessmen see these things and are able to plan ahead. Also, when people come to trust you on a higher level, they will make better deals with you, and even introduce you to more and better connections. Indeed, it is not all about money.

V

The Power of Prayer

When I was in grade school, I remember whenever my mother visited a supplier or went to see a buyer, she would ask me to go with her. I was typically shy. Therefore, I would reason that I could just wait in the car with the driver because there was nothing I could do for her. She would reply, saying, "You don't have to do anything. Just watch." Really, that was a trick. I realized later in my adulthood those ordinary experiences had shaped my perception of people and the world around me. My mother had trained me to be an entrepreneur.

The shellcraft-handicraft industry in Cebu, Philippines was a large network of small businesses. There were people doing the shell beads business, there were those doing only shell toys (small seashells creatively assembled to form decorative pieces that resembled toys), there were those doing only shell placemats (typically using cowrie shells and nassarius beads to form small mats and coasters), and there were those dealing only with raw seashells cleaned and polished for interested seashell collectors, to name a few.

In the shell beads business alone, there were shops who specialized in heishi beads, there were a few who specialized in the production of trocha shells or cone shells into a variety of bead shapes, or the production of cleaned, polished, and strung small shells to accent fashion necklaces and accessories. Each businessman or artisan would be dedicated to providing this particular product from among the myriad of possible products one could choose to do. What struck me as interesting was the passion each person had as a maker of his or her product. Another thing that awed me was the opportunity this person had when he or she went to business with this particular product.

In those many years of exposure to workers, artisans and small businesses, it was not surprising to me anymore whenever my parent and I would seek to find a supplier in the remotest place, and the supplier would express that we were an answered prayer. It could even be in a situation where the supplier was already planning to close their shop or the supplier had a financial need to provide for family. That prayer was answered. Sometimes, it was the other way around. Sometimes, a particular buyer came to find us because my parents had prayed ardently too.

Despite the hard times that come and go, there are small businesses that thrive because enough customers have come to buy their products, allowing them to continually operate, and because these small business owners have kept passion in their hearts. Certain people are led to the store to buy, and certain business opportunities come to happen, at times in unexpected ways. Perhaps because there is a purpose for all of these. That purpose makes it possible to meet the right people at the right place and at the right time.

When I began to see business endeavour as a life's purpose, I began to understand the reason why businesses continue to provide a product or service in spite of the challenges the owners have along the way. I also began to understand why those opportunities, which could be life-changing, happen along with prayers. There is a Higher Being up there who makes all these possible for the grander scheme of things.

VI

What Hat Do You Wear?

There was a joke inside our house one time about "Yes, Sir, my mother dyed." A buyer had called to follow-up if my parents were going to deliver the cocoshell beads (beads made from coconut shell) which he specified to be in this certain shade of blue. One should not make the mistake of coloring it too dark or too light of a blue. No wonder why after a few trials and errors, my mother decided to do it herself to find the perfect mixture. Those bead strands were now soaking, so I assured the buyer, "Yes, Sir, my mother dyed already." It was hilarious when I related the story to my parents. Dyed, not died, as those two were pronounced the same.

In small business, it is very common -- inevitable even -- that the owner will perform many roles. At times it is a matter of pure interest; at other times, it is for survival. In my parents' business card, it listed my mother as proprietor and my father as manager. But, of course, they were both proprietors and managers of the company. My father was good at organizing documents, files and payrolls, so it was natural that he was managing these things. My mother was a good saleswoman who could engage the clients in entertaining conversations and get them happily convinced to buy. So, my father would often tell a prospective buyer to wait until my mother arrived. My father was disciplined with his time, while my mother was taking hers. Which worked, depending on the situations.

A happy memory that my mother and I shared was when they were still starting in the business, and my mother had to string the beads herself to make initial samples to customers, which would take until midnight. I was a small girl then and I would not go to bed without her. So, I would sleepily sit on the table and wait for her, and watch. Until I took interest in copying her and strung some beads and made my own design so I wouldn't fall asleep waiting. When you start something from scratch, you get to learn every step. My mother was a designer, purchaser, saleswoman, human resource person and production-in-charge rolled into one. It was a practical thing for small business owners like her to wear many hats because it helped minimize the cost of production or cost of operation. When you bring the final product to the table, with the lesser cost, you have better capacity to compete with price or the better your final profit (net profit) will be. This is helpful especially when the business is just starting, so you can add more capital to the business to help it grow.

What hat do you wear?

VII

Blending Traditional Ways With Modern Ways

There was a time in the 1990s when the shellcraft-handicraft fashion industry in Cebu had some sort of renaissance. Many new exporters emerged. Most carried with them years of corporate experience and business degrees. However, in less than a decade, many of those new companies closed down because they could not meet operational costs when orders from foreign buyers started to dwindle.

I had grown up in an environment where businesses were run in the traditional way. When we needed the help of our worker to put clasps in the shell necklaces fast enough so we could meet production time, the woman would assemble her children to get the job done. It was common to see production done in the backyard of homes and family members putting in their share of labor, even if it was something as simple as putting items inside boxes to pack. These were the old businesses -- manufacturers, wholesalers and exporters -- who remained resilient despite economic downturns.

I had seen as common mistake made by those starting new business was the tendency to spend more rather than bootstrap. While being forward-thinking and adaptive is commendable in modern businesses, surely there are things that can be learned from traditional businesses too -- that is, how they value relationships and how they utilize resources available in the most inexpensive ways.

Needless to say, if traditional businesses were more forward-thinking and adaptive to newer trends, they could have experienced more growth in the business. Like what I had seen among a few of my parents' contemporaries, who later owned store and hotel chains or several other lucrative businesses, or went to supply to bigger clients.

VIII

Starting Business From Scratch

Because I grew up in small business, often I am asked for advice how to start one. I generally say, choose one that you find interesting enough to devote time and energy to, before it starts earning money.

Identify what type of business you want to be in -- if it is manufacturing, wholesaling or retailing. When you start a product, try it on a small segment of your target customers first. Use the feedbacks from customers to keep improving the product. As you improve your product and get more customers, you are also increasing your capacity to deliver more. Do not jump to large-scale operations without the proper preparation that will be required by it.

It is laudable to be a dreamer when you are building something, but be humble too, somebody who is easy to work with. You will need it when you approach prospect buyers and suppliers. Also, recognize there are government agencies and organizations that will be supportive of your goals and you can seek help from them.

I got my biggest client, a large chain store in the United States, in 2008. It was a goal I had in mind for many years. That was why I approached a retail store to show my samples a decade before. I started with an order of 6 pieces of each style, then because the products sold well, the store owner increased the order to 12 pieces of each style. Then I approached another retail store with more outlets, and got an order of 24 pieces of each style, and then more. The product underwent modifications in form and function and in packaging. What I learned about producing and marketing one product helped me in starting another product. Having built the experience and met the expectations of my clients, I ultimately found myself ready to take on my dream client.

Starting business from scratch

IX

Coming Full Circle

In their later years, my parents were selling shell and wood bead strands from their stall in the handicraft market. Every day they would go to the stall to personally take charge. They were done with travelling to their clients and selling in trade shows. They preferred the lower stress involved while doing wholesale-retail from their small shop as compared to having to meet strict shipment deadlines and rigorous quality controls during exporting in their heyday. They now enjoyed the opportunity to interact with both customers and suppliers when they came to the shop. They also felt camaraderie with other stall owners, which gave them a sense of belonging. Things were back to being simpler. That kind of transition came so naturally for them and seemed to feel just right. After all those many adventures in the business and in life.

At that point, my parents might have thought they did not accomplish much. But, I would say, they actually did. The business had provided for our family's needs. We had been living on a 2,500-square-meter property. They had an islet and built a cottage on it. For the most part of their lives, they had employed people or helped suppliers who were able to support their families. If my parents took another road along their journey, or navigated different waters, we do not know if they would have done better or less. Nevertheless, their small business was not only a livelihood for them; it was their life. Their business endeavours had truly enriched their personal experiences.

In the end, they might not have built an empire nor felt they found their "holy grail," as many small businesses are also inclined to view of themselves later on. But having the freedom to be what they wanted to be in the business and the freedom to keep the business in the size that did not have to stress them so much is I think the holy grail itself.

END

AUTHOR'S BIO

Ma. Catherine Ymbong-Ancheta lives in Calgary, Alberta, Canada with her husband Sonny and their three sons Francis, Gabriel and Russell.

She had completed Harvard Business School Online Certificate Program, "Entrepreneurship Essentials," in 2019.

www.ingramcontent.com/pod-product-compliance
Lightning Source LLC
Chambersburg PA
CBHW031555210526
45464CB00003B/1301